SEE IT GROW!

See a Banana Grow

by Kirsten Chang

BELLWETHER MEDIA · MINNEAPOLIS, MN

Blastoff! Readers are carefully developed by literacy experts to build reading stamina and move students toward fluency by combining standards-based content with developmentally appropriate text.

Level 1 provides the most support through repetition of high-frequency words, light text, predictable sentence patterns, and strong visual support.

Level 2 offers early readers a bit more challenge through varied sentences, increased text load, and text-supportive special features.

Level 3 advances early-fluent readers toward fluency through increased text load, less reliance on photos, advancing concepts, longer sentences, and more complex special features.

★ **Blastoff! Universe**

Reading Level

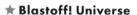

Grade **K**

Grades **1–3**

Grade **4**

This edition first published in 2023 by Bellwether Media, Inc.

No part of this publication may be reproduced in whole or in part without written permission of the publisher. For information regarding permission, write to Bellwether Media, Inc., Attention: Permissions Department, 6012 Blue Circle Drive, Minnetonka, MN 55343.

Library of Congress Cataloging-in-Publication Data

LC record for See a Banana Grow available at http://lccn.loc.gov/2022039513

Editor: Betsy Rathburn   Designer: Brittany McIntosh

Printed in the United States of America, North Mankato, MN.

Table of **Contents**

Tasty Fruits   4

How Do They Grow?   6

Fully Grown   18

Glossary   22

To Learn More   23

Index   24

Tasty Fruits

We are eating bananas. These fruits grow in the **tropics**!

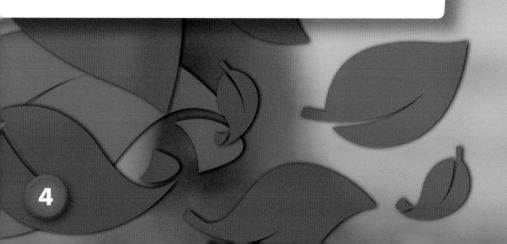

4

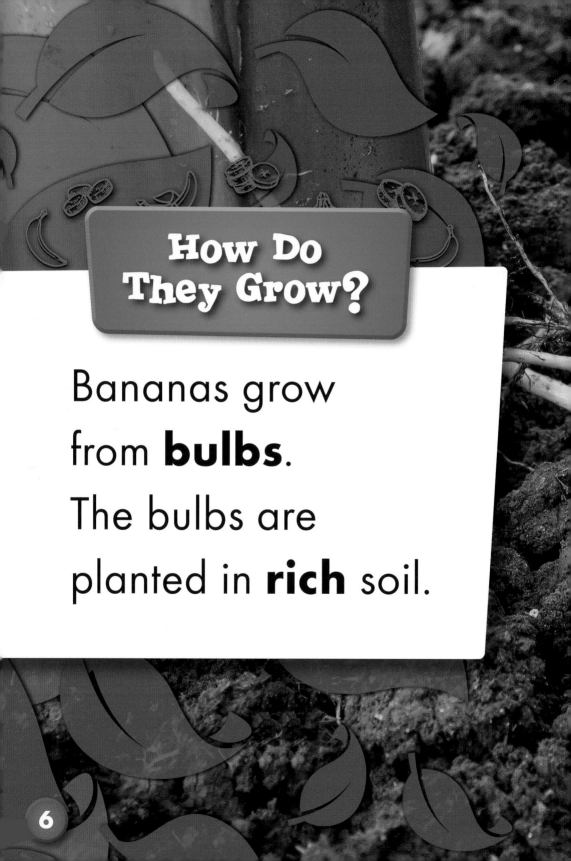

How Do They Grow?

Bananas grow from **bulbs**. The bulbs are planted in **rich** soil.

bulb

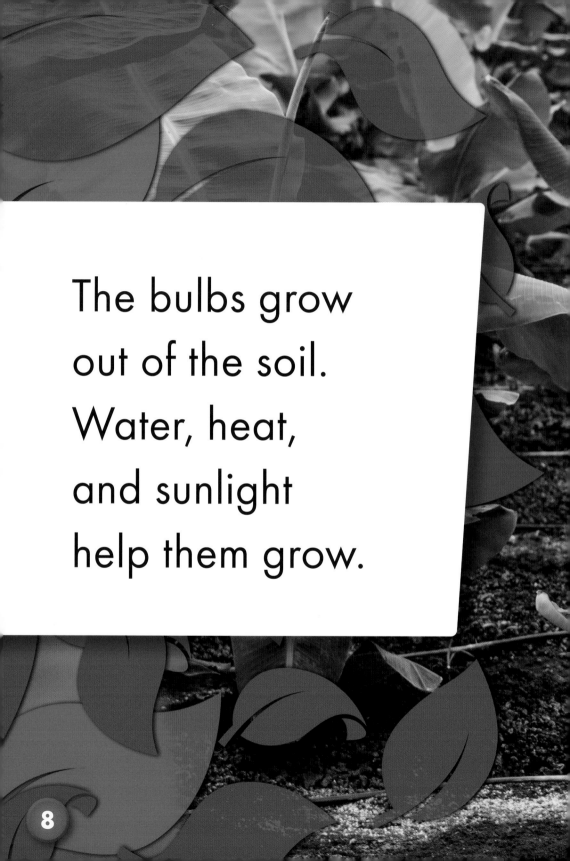

The bulbs grow
out of the soil.
Water, heat,
and sunlight
help them grow.

Needed to Grow

rich soil

water

heat and sunlight

The plants grow
tall **stalks**.
Their **buds** open.
Tiny flowers
are inside!

flowers

bud

stalk

The flowers grow into **bunches** of bananas.

banana
bunches

The bananas
are green.
Farm workers
pick them.

picking
bananas

The stalk is cut down.
A new plant grows!

Fully Grown

Bananas turn yellow when they are ready to eat.

Using Bananas

banana
bread

banana
cream pie

banana
pancakes

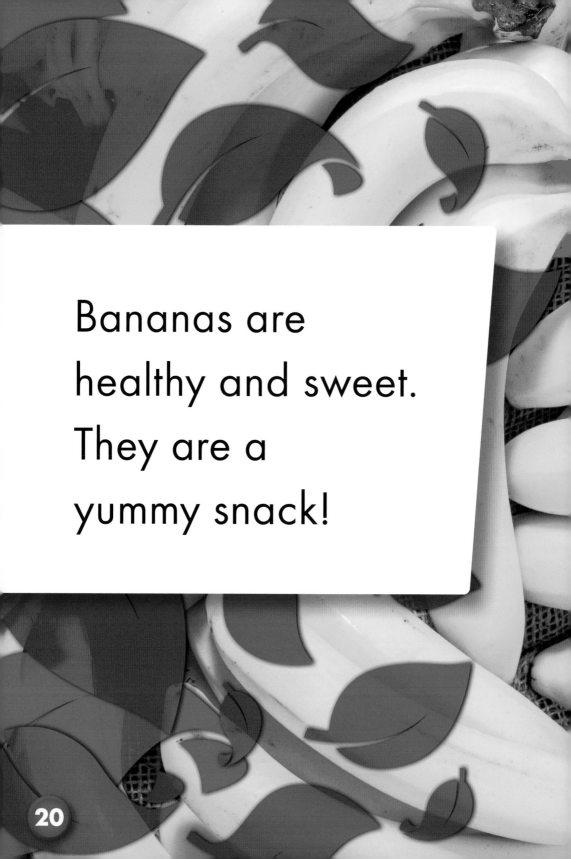

Bananas are
healthy and sweet.
They are a
yummy snack!

Banana Life Cycle

1 bulb is planted in rich soil

2 bulb grows into a tall stalk with flowers

3 flowers grow into bananas

4 stalk is cut down to the bulb

Glossary

buds

growths that turn into flowers

rich

full of the things plants need to grow

bulbs

parts of some plants that form underground and grow new plants

stalks

long, skinny parts of some plants that grow leaves and flowers

bunches

groups of bananas that grow together

tropics

hot parts of the world

To Learn More

AT THE LIBRARY

Brannon, Cecelia H. *Bananas*. New York, N.Y.: Enslow Publishing, 2018.

Chang, Kirsten. *See a Pumpkin Grow*. Minneapolis, Minn.: Bellwether Media, 2023.

Connors, Kathleen. *How Do Bananas Grow?* New York, N.Y.: Gareth Stevens Publishing, 2021.

ON THE WEB

FACTSURFER

Factsurfer.com gives you a safe, fun way to find more information.

1. Go to www.factsurfer.com.

2. Enter "see a banana grow" into the search box and click 🔍.

3. Select your book cover to see a list of related content.

Index

buds, 10, 11

bulbs, 6, 7, 8

bunches, 12, 13

eat, 4, 18

farm workers, 14

flowers, 10, 11, 12

fruits, 4

green, 14

heat, 8

life cycle, 21

needed to grow, 9

snack, 20

soil, 6, 8

stalks, 10, 11, 16

sunlight, 8

tropics, 4

using bananas, 19

water, 8

yellow, 18

The images in this book are reproduced through the courtesy of: Amor Kar, front cover (seed); nuwatphoto, front cover (seedling); somyot pattana, front cover (banana); Superheang168, p. 3; PAPA WOR, pp. 4-5; Gheorghe Mindru, pp. 6-7, 22 (bulbs); Parikh Mahendra N, pp. 8-9; nito, p. 9 (top left); Martin Valigursky, p. 9 (top middle); Andrey Danilovich, p. 9 (top right); panda3800, pp. 10-11; TigerStocks, p. 11 (top); BoonmeeKim, pp. 12-13; ThitareeSarmkasat, pp. 14-15; TA BLUE Capture, pp. 16-17; Luis Echeverri Urrea, pp. 18-19; Shutter B Photo, p. 19 (bottom left); Pixel-Shot, p. 19 (bottom middle); Africa Studio, p. 19 (bottom right); Hanna_photo, pp. 20-21; KobchaiMa, p. 22 (buds); Baloncici, p. 22 (bunches); kram-9, p. 22 (rich); sunsetman, p. 22 (stalks); PuwanaiSomwanPhoto, p. 22 (tropics); Nataly Studio, p. 23.